THE
LEADING
EDGE

THE
HAGGAI
INSTITUTE
STORY

John Edmund Haggai

Kobrey Books
Atlanta, Georgia

For information write:
Dr. John Edmund Haggai
Haggai Institute
P.O. Box 13
Atlanta, Georgia 30370
USA

ISBN 1-883108-05-5

Design by Stephen Lown **Graphic Designer**

Contents

Preface

When Paul G. Hiebert, served as professor of missions and anthropology at the School of World Missions, he wrote the following words:

By taking mature, established leaders from around the world, Haggai Institute has cut the time and cost needed to train people, and built upon those of proven and trusted abilities. By training lay leaders for ministries in the Church, it is working to mobilize the whole of the Church, and has avoided a dependency on Western-style ministerial roles that have not worked well in many cultures where the Church is found. By working with those already in established careers, the Institute has escaped the problems of colonial paternalism and foreign dependency that plague the modern missions scene, and has built a network of fellowship and equality among Church leaders around the world.

I am a grateful second-generation product of Western colonial missions. Western missionaries served the Lord sacrificially to the eternal benefit of my family. But today is a new day, with new challenges. And these new challenges require new methods – methods that put Haggai Institute at the leading edge of world missions.

This book tells the Haggai Institute story and explains why Haggai Institute remains unique in its approach. Many men and women of energy and vision have played a part in establishing the work. Some of them are featured in the pages that follow. That many have not received a mention is explained by the fact that this volume goes out mainly as an orientation tool for participants and was not designed to be an exhaustive history of the organization.

The emphasis of Haggai Institute's work remains that of leveraging the Gospel message outreach. Unlike many other groups, we do not accomplish this through telecommunications. We thank God for the way He is using all forms of media. But we also believe in the unique power of personal contact and the vital importance of men and women hearing the Gospel in their own cultural context, from those who in every sense "speak their language."

From such a premise the whole vision of Haggai Institute sprang. ∎

Introduction:
Why Haggai Institute?

There is a problem with preaching the Gospel, and it goes right back to the New Testament.

As every Bible student knows, the last thing Jesus did before He ascended was to give His disciples the Great Commission: "Go therefore and make disciples of all nations, baptizing them in the name of the Father and of the Son and of the Holy Spirit..." (Matthew 28:19).

And they did. In fact, all the way from Jesus' time to our own, men and women have been sacrificing their comforts – and often their lives – to "go and make disciples." Paul the Apostle, Columba, Francis Xavier, Mary Slessor, J. Hudson Taylor, David Livingstone – we admire such people precisely because they went to the ends of the earth for the Gospel. Not surprisingly, then, our ideas of "successful missions" are shaped by them. I personally have every reason to be grateful, for if missionaries hadn't brought my father's family to Christ all those years ago in Damascus, Syria, I wouldn't even have been born.

So what's the problem? Well, in a nutshell we could put it like this: *Modern missionary work makes a lot more of "going" than it does of "making disciples."*

Many Western Christians have attended presentations where a dedicated missionary couple home on furlough share the unrelenting struggle by which they've squeezed out a meager handful of conversions. Almost always our response is to affirm them, to pat them on the back and say, "Well done. I wish I had the courage to do what you do. Keep at it." Nobody asks why their productivity is so low. Never mind that they've come back practically empty-handed – the point is that they *went*.

David Livingstone

Is this really what Jesus meant by "going out and making disciples"? Certainly no one applies this kind of reasoning in business. You can do all the "going" you want in marketing, but if you don't come back with a sale, you've done nothing but run up hotel bills. "Go and make disciples" means exactly what it says. God doesn't mock us with impossible standards. If we're not making disciples, then it's time we sat down and figured out why not. I don't think you have to look far to see what's wrong. In today's global environment, the traditional model of missions has three glaring weaknesses:

1. CULTURE. Missionaries are foreigners. Their knowledge of local culture is limited; sometimes they can barely speak the language. Ask yourself: Is that the kind of person most likely to persuade you? It's no insult to the Holy Spirit to observe that we react most positively to those whose background we share. Besides which, turn up at many airports with the word *missionary* in your passport and you won't even get in. More than 70 percent of those in Asia, Africa, and Latin America live in nations where preaching by Western missionaries is restricted or prohibited. The Arab world is closed to Western missionaries. So too are the world's two largest nations, India and the People's Republic of China. If preaching the Gospel in these lands depends on missionaries, that's a lot of people not hearing the Gospel.

2. MONEY. Sending missionaries is expensive. Once you've factored in air fares, accommodation and living expenses, keeping just one missionary couple on site for a year won't leave you much change out of $100,000. There will never be enough missionaries even to make a dent on global unbelief. And "the nations" are growing with every passing hour. In a year, world population increases by almost 100 million. Over the same period, the Churches record maybe 7 million conversions. At this rate we're nowhere near evangelizing the globe. We're losing ground fast.

3. POWER. Unfortunately, Western missionary work often has been confused with colonial expansion.

In a year, world population increases by almost 100 million...

William Carey, for instance, went to India in the wake of the British East India Company. The "white man's religion" therefore came in the same basket as the white man's technology, goods, medicine, learning, and culture. This has had a curious effect. On the one hand, in countries where nationalism is strong, the Gospel will often be seen as "foreign" and rejected for that reason alone. On the other hand, there is a tendency for Christians, particularly in America, to see world evangelism as basically "their responsibility." They are reluctant to hand over control, and so they perpetuate a culture of dependency in which their "support" of missions overseas actually undermines the Gospel. In forty years I can honestly tell you I've never seen Western funding produce a strong, local non-Western Church. An American once boasted to me that he'd financed 40 overseas Churches. Later he mournfully confided that none of them had prospered.

Let's be honest. If we were starting from scratch, we wouldn't evangelize the globe by sending out a small group of expensive and ill-acclimatized Westerners. It's inefficient, it's costly, and in most situations, it makes no sense. The world has changed; our way of obeying the Great Commission has to change with it.

So Haggai Institute is a response to changing times. We take with absolute seriousness Jesus' command to "make disciples of all the nations." We also argue that "going" to make disciples is not as simple as it seems. In the new global environment, *effective* preaching of the Gospel must recognize three things:

...over the same period, the Churches record maybe 7 million conversions.

1. The people best equipped to communicate the Gospel are those who share the culture and nationality of their audience.

2. Effective communication of the Gospel on a global scale requires the mobilizing of a large missionary force.

3. Mobilizing that force demands fresh initiatives under God, with leadership-skilled Christians worldwide as key players.

Haggai Institute has built its missions strategy on precisely this foundation.

We don't send anyone out (although the total number of people now preaching in response to our program far exceeds the largest denominational mission force). Nor do we undertake social or humanitarian projects (though many of our alumni have scored huge successes in these areas). What we do is *promote the crucial Christian leadership skills by which influential Christians can become effective evangelists.*

The pedigree of the H.I. program is attested by both the quality of our alumni – many of them are in the very top positions – and by the evangelistic work they've done since returning to their own countries. All our participants come to us as credentialed leaders – business, civic, professional, and religious. All those attending international seminars do so at one of our two training facilities strategically located in Singapore and Maui. And all work with a top-flight faculty drawn mainly from the non-West, who are, in turn, responsible for generating the training materials.

By the grace and providence of God, no other ministry provides such a high level of input to such a high level of leadership. No other ministry has a comparable track record. No other ministry is active in as many non-Western nations, or has so completely avoided the trap of re-inventing colonial missions by doling out "Western expertise." Even the funding for Haggai Institute is quickly becoming global. H.I. India now runs and finances itself, and one of the largest recent donations to the international program has come from a supporter in Indonesia.

Why does the method work? Simply because it utilizes the principle of leverage. Many years ago, I absorbed the maxim: *He who does the work is not so profitably employed as he who multiplies the workers.*

Thus participants gain entry to H.I. sessions only if they undertake to train at least a hundred others within two years of their return to their own countries. We know that our alumni honor this pledge; indeed some train multiple hundreds and even thousands. From the 43,000 directly trained by H.I., therefore, we realize a "leveraged" mission force numbering in the millions.

People sometimes ask why we keep such a low profile. The answer is simple: turning H.I. into a headline ministry would cause difficulties to those alumni operating in politically sensitive areas, and make it harder for many future participants to get clearance for travel overseas. Even granted this limitation, however, the work grows apace. Even after the introduction of regional seminars, demand for the program continually outstrips our capacity to provide training places, and Haggai Institute has prayerfully planned to stay on the leading edge of missions until Christ returns. ■

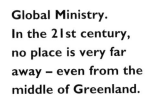

Global Ministry. In the 21st century, no place is very far away – even from the middle of Greenland.

1 Chinese Whispers

As a boy, I loved missions. The problem was, I didn't want to ruin myself by becoming a minister.

Ministry at that time was far from being a glamorous vocation. Most clergy seemed to live in run-down parsonages and survive on near poverty-level wages. I knew that first-hand – my father was one of them. More than a few times I saw this man's superior talents go unrewarded. More than a few times I saw him distressed when our straitened finances prevented his giving us children some of the things our neighbors enjoyed.

I didn't want to get into that position. So when in 1937, I scored top marks for business ability in aptitude tests sponsored by the New York Regents, my way forward seemed clear. *Aha,* I thought to myself, *I'll be the best businessman I can be, and I'll support a hundred missionaries.*

The roadster rolls over

Then something happened that changed my mind in a hurry.

It was the day after Christmas, 1940, when I was sixteen years old. My friend and I were riding together in his roadster. It was the only time in my life I can remember telling anyone to slow down. Unfortunately I did it too late. He turned sharply on ice and lost control. The car rolled over. The flying windshield nearly severed my leg.

Strong family roots. A rare photograph showing me (left), TOM (center) and TED (right) with our beloved parents.

For eight months I was off my feet. The doctors couldn't even guarantee I'd keep the leg, let alone walk with it. On top of that, the treatment required mega-doses of sulfanilamide. The best medical opinion available at the time told me sulfanilamide would deplete my white blood cell count, resulting in leukemia and an early death – probably before I reached forty.

Most compelling, shortly after I arrived at the hospital I heard the doctors whispering, *"The lad may not make it until daybreak."* Facing death put my priorities in order fast. Right there I determined to give my life to the will of the Lord. Business went out the window. It wasn't that making money was evil – it's good, even divine, if God has called you to it. But I knew it wasn't what He wanted for me.

After graduating from high school, I enrolled at Moody Bible Institute and got the basics for the Gospel ministry. Many of the sermons I heard, though, were little more than pleasant Sunday morning essays, and it took some powerful preaching – and some giants of the pulpit – to show me what ministry could be. Dr. Robert G. Lee, Bishop John Taylor Smith, Dr. J.C. Massee, Dr. W. B. Riley, Dr. Porter Barrington, Dr. Harold Fickett, and Dr. R.S. Beal – these would hold me spellbound. And for gripping Bible teaching, nobody got my attention like my own father.

When my call arrived, however, it came not through a church pastor, but through a missionary. Long before I did the aptitude test, I'd been fascinated by Christian work in China. And missionaries like Paul Metzler and Carl Tanis had re-awakened the desire to see the Gospel preached on a global footing. But it was Paul Fleming, founder of New Tribes Mission, whose challenge from the pulpit spoke straight to my heart.

"Don't be a hypocrite," he said. *"Don't say you are waiting for the Lord to lead you to the mission field.*

Facing death put my priorities in order fast.

3

How are you going to know His leading? Assume that He wants you to go to the foreign missionary field unless He closes the door."

Wow – that hit home!

Suddenly my childhood love for China set into a rock-firm ambition to contribute to evangelizing that huge nation. And then – out of the blue – everything got turned on its head. In 1949 Mao's revolution slammed the door shut. Americans were thrown out. Missionaries were expelled. And with no obvious route to pursue my missionary calling, I was stuck on my own doorstep – facing a call to the pulpit of a local Church.

Mission from America

I stayed in the pastoral ministry for twelve years. I served Churches in Pekin, Illinois; Lancaster, South Carolina; Chattanooga, Tennessee; and Louisville, Kentucky. God blessed those ministries. And in a strange way, my earlier plan to support missions through business found fulfillment. I did everything I could to support the overseas missionary effort, and each congregation blazed a trail in missions giving.

Second Baptist in Lancaster, had released less than a thousand dollars for missions in 1948. In my first full year there, missions giving increased by a factor of twenty-seven. Over a similar period at my last pastorate, Ninth and O Baptist Church in Louisville, the missions budget swelled by 650 percent. Missions support became the priority passion of my heart.

In addition, local Church ministry provided a tremendous training ground. I learned the craft of prospecting, recruiting, and fund-raising. But even the fact that Ninth and O led the 11 leading evangelical denominations in numbers of converts and baptisms didn't excite me as it might have done.

EDWARD YU. Formerly the President of the New South Wales Baptist Union in Sydney, Australia, this China-born minister joined Haggai Institute in 1995, later becoming H.I.'s Vice President for Asia.

The haunting words of Canadian missionary statesman Oswald J. Smith kept goading me: *Why should anybody hear the Gospel twice until everybody has heard it once?* Deep in my heart I knew I would never feel fulfilled until, like John Wesley, I was working directly in world evangelism.

During my last 18 months in Louisville, Kentucky, my final pastorate, I received over 400 invitations to conduct evangelistic meetings, both local and citywide. Sensing in this a divine call I could not ignore – and with the thorough cooperation of Christine, my wife, and my invalid son, Johnny – I embarked upon an evangelistic ministry that began in 1957 and continued into the 1970s.

These included meetings at such Churches as the Bellevue Baptist in Memphis, Tennessee, the Tremont Temple Baptist Church in Boston, Massachusetts, the Moody Church in Chicago, Illinois, the Church of the Open Door in Los Angeles, the Young Nak Presbyterian Church in Seoul, Korea, and the Copacabana Presbyterian Church in Rio de Janeiro.

A poster from one of the many citywide crusades God used to reach America around 1960.

Within the five months of going into evangelism, I conducted my first citywide crusade at the Ladd Stadium in Mobile, Alabama. By late 1968 I had begun to move overseas – first to Jakarta, Indonesia and then to Beirut, Lebanon (1969) and Lisbon, Portugal (1972). These crusades, particularly the ones in Asia, sharpened the razor of my desire to serve God in worldwide missions.

But how was I to move on? ■

Aldo Fontao ARGENTINA

Aldo Fontao's accomplishments are many: leading cardiologist, pastor of the largest church in his denomination, Moderator of the Presbyterian Church of Argentina.

And yet, says Aldo, *"Before I went to Haggai Institute at Singapore I had not led a single person to the Lord. Since then I have led many. The Haggai Institute training is the basis of everything I do now. I have reprocessed the material and am using it in all areas of my work."*

He sets himself clear goals, which he inevitably attains – twenty people to be trained in church administration at a Bible institute, a group of young people to be prepared for pastoral leadership. Haggai Institute's principles of goal-setting have even found their way into Aldo's lectures on cardiovascular physiology at Argentina's biggest university in Buenos Aires.

Unusually, Aldo directs part of his ministry to the wealthy. *"You need the right profile to attract high executives and professionals. I help them set goals. I also have a counseling committee which includes managers of some of the big enterprises."*

He's also involved in the ministry of healing. Three cancer cases were healed recently in his church. And this leading physician knows his medical expertise played no part. *"The Lord did it,"* he says. *"I'm just an instrument."*

Dr. Fontao now serves as Vice President, Training and Development, Maui.

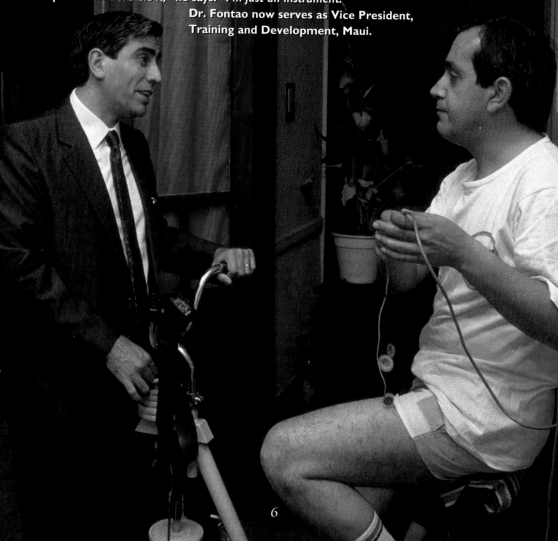

2 What Began in Beirut

It's been said that success in local Church ministry links directly to the depth of the leader's prayer life, the number of hours he labors, and his ability to work with people.

On all three fronts, I endeavored to give 110 percent. From August 1945 until the end of 1964, in fact, I worked continually, seven days a week. Throughout that period I enjoyed the love and support of my wife Christine. But events beyond our control soon put us under severe strain. Our son Johnny had suffered birth injuries at the hands of an incompetent and drunken surgeon, and was left with cerebral palsy. As if that were not hard enough to bear, Johnny's needs kept Chris confined to the house around the clock. I was being torn apart, wanting to be with them, but knowing that my ministry didn't allow me the luxury of staying at home.

With JOHNNY, who, in his brief 24 years, gave the ministry so much devoted prayer, encouragement and support.

And then St. Andrews University in Scotland invited me to speak to their faculty and graduate students. Accepting the assignment seemed impossible. I was booked up for the next two years. And how could I leave town, let alone leave the country, without placing an intolerable burden on Chris? Chris, though, saw things differently, and she spoke up. *"If you don't take a break,"* she said, *"you're going to kill yourself. And where will that leave Johnny and me?"* Then she added. *"Why don't you take that trip to Scotland? And when you're finished at St. Andrews, go to the Middle East, and visit the land of your fathers. Why don't you go over Christmas and New Year's?"*

The next day I arranged a three-week tour, to begin mid-December at St. Andrews and conclude in early January.

The developing nations – close up

Like many at that time, I assumed America was a place the developing nations looked to with envy – a place of freedom, opportunity, and wealth. That was why my father had come from Damascus back in 1912. It stood to reason, then, that Americans and American influence would be welcomed. Or so I thought.

To my surprise, many in the developing world had lost confidence in America. True, they didn't want Soviet communism; but they didn't want American capitalism, either. They wanted independence. Traveling through the Middle East, the repercussions quickly dawned on me. First, nationalist agendas would soon lead to Westerners being restricted, even barred, in many areas of the world, just as they'd been already in China. And second, in order to work with this new geopolitics, *the Church would have to adopt a very different approach to missions.*

One event, in particular, transformed my thinking almost overnight.

"They treat us like children..."

I'd arrived in Lebanon to find a thriving Christian community. Though my citizenship and commitment are 100 percent American, my bloodlines go back on my mother's side to England, and on my father's to Syria. I was "in the middle" in more ways than one. Consequently, Middle Eastern nationals confronted me with an earnest plea.

"John," they said. *"We love the missionaries, but they treat us like children. We are not satisfied to be marionettes on the end of a Western string. That offends us. The work of God suffers because we are not treated as equals. The missionaries love us; they're*

MICHAEL YOUSSEF. Rector of Atlanta's Church of the Apostles, and Founder of Leading the Way Ministries, Dr. Michael Youssef gave ten years to H.I. and remains one of its most valued advisors.

willing to die for us, but they are not willing to share the ministry."

That stung. Frankly, it made me angry. I told them what a crucial role the missionaries had played in my father's escape from the barbaric oppression of Turkey's Ottoman Empire. I reminded them of the enormous sacrifices missionaries had made – that in the 167 years to 1960, one out of every four members of missionary families in India had died in foreign service. How could they question the methods of those willing to pay such a high price for their commitment? *"And they love you so much,"* I argued.

"No, no, no, habibi," they insisted (*habibi* is a term of endearment). *"Please don't be upset. But the truth is, people of high intellect and high position are not willing to let young foreigners set the agenda, deploy the leadership personnel and, in short, call the shots. They aren't rejecting Jesus. They're rejecting Western domination."*

Clearly much of this had already been said to the missionaries. Three days later, the heads of the thirteen major mission organizations in Lebanon, including my own, the Southern Baptist, invited me to a testimonial dinner in my honor. At first I thought it was a "roast" and was preparing myself for that uniquely American experience of having some good-humored jokes told at my expense. But they were serious. *"Haggai,"* they said, *"tell your camel-jockey cousins we can't hand everything over to them willy-nilly. We have accountability to our denominational boards back home in Nashville, Springfield, and Dallas."*

So that was the dilemma. The fire of nationalism was sweeping through the Middle East. Indeed, it was sweeping across the entire globe. In the nineteen years since the end of Word War II, more than a hundred new nations had emerged and

KEITH CHUA. This Singapore Chinese Christian leader serves as chairman of the Singapore Board. Despite heavy commitments in hotels, property development and finance, he and his wife Irene make a powerful contribution to the H.I. ministry both in the East and the West.

patriotic zeal had soared to a new height. Meanwhile the missionaries – many of whom, I'm sure, knew perfectly well what was going on – had behind them American mission boards steeped in nineteenth-century methods.

The result? These new nationalists perceived these dedicated efforts to preach the Gospel of Christ as foreign interference. Missions were failing to adapt to changing times – and the dissemination of the Gospel was suffering.

Surely someone's thought of this before?

RONNIE IRVINE. A businessman in Northern Ireland, Ronnie Irvine has lent his considerable talents to H.I. both as a board member and as H.I.'s representative in the U.K.

Have you ever had an idea that's so obvious, so simple, that you thought: *If there were any value in this, surely someone would have acted on it by now?* That's what was going through my mind as I flew across the Mediterranean on my return to the United States. I was convinced I must be missing something, convinced that the men and women in charge of missions policy had noted the problem and were working fervently to solve it.

I was wrong.

Over the next few months I talked with many leaders about the challenge of international evangelism. I listened hard to what they had to say. And almost every one of them – in the denominations and parachurch groups alike – held the same view of missions. It boiled down to this. You take a Western volunteer. You put John 3:16 in his right hand, and the song *Jesus Loves Me* in his left. And then you send him out to reach the lowest socioeconomic levels of the non-Western world.

The whole mindset of missions was stuck in a bygone era. It no longer addressed real needs. I applauded the dedication of Western mission groups. They were, and are, led by conscientious people with sincere aims. But the assumptions they worked from were obsolete. By the mid-1960s, Christians concerned with the developing world fell into one of two groups:

1. Those committed to social service, who believed that others would accept Christ if the missionaries improved living conditions and showed Christ-like compassion.

2. Those committed to evangelism, who believed the success of missions in a given country was in direct proportion to the number of Western missionaries working within its borders.

Even then, perceptive leaders in world evangelism saw clearly that, *as a way of obeying the Great Commission,* neither made much impact. And the reason lay not in the resources Western Churches put into missions, but in the way missions were organized and understood. I never heard the problem more precisely summed up than by Fred Thomas, an Indonesian alumnus of Haggai Institute, who told me in 1979: *"Many people in the West are willing to sacrifice their lives for the sake of the Gospel. But they are not willing to sacrifice their thoughts."*

GEORGE SAMUEL. Previously a research scientist for the Indian government and consultant to the UN, George Samuel has distinguished himself as dean of H.I.

Shattering the glass walls

Researchers once performed an experiment on Japanese fighting fish. A tank was constructed with a glass divider in the middle. On one side the researchers placed the fighting fish; on the other side, the fish they normally fed on. At first the predators launched themselves again and again at their prey – only to smack against the divider. Finally they gave up. And when the next day the researchers removed the glass wall, an interesting thing happened. Instead of rushing over and devouring their prey, the predatory fish stayed where they were. Nothing now prevented them from crossing into the other half of the tank – the limitations were entirely self-imposed.

Something like this had happened to Western missions. You'd think that the "low performance" of missionaries would have prompted a radical reappraisal of missionary methods. In fact, the opposite had occurred. Instead of challenging the *concept* of sending Westerners out to preach in unfamiliar cultures, people began to see missionaries as both underdogs and heroes.

I think of an American missionary couple I heard speaking on furlough, telling of their twenty-seven years in a strange land. They'd endured an oppressive climate without the aid of air-conditioning, and tolerated unfamiliar food. They'd struggled with the elements of nature, even as they'd struggled to master the language and to understand

P.K.D. Lee INDIA

P.K.D. Lee came to Christ in the midst of an illustrious career which has included senior positions in the Indian Railways and a spell as General Manager of the Indian government mint.

He soon became a zealous evangelist and a dedicated church leader, seeking to preach the Gospel where Hinduism and Islam are dominant. His visit to Haggai Institute in 1979 immediately transformed his approach to witnessing. He wrote shortly afterwards to say, "I have changed my method of presenting the Gospel such that, when I last traveled about India, many Hindus I spoke with said they have never heard the Gospel presented so clearly."

P.K.D. Lee has played a leading role in the development of H.I. India. He has led the Haggai Institute work in the subcontinent to self-support under Indian alumni. In 1999 this gifted leader and communicator moved on to serve as Haggai Institute's executive director for international advancement.

the society. They lamented that age had now put an end to their missionary service, and reported with great joy and thanks to God that in their final stint they'd seen *two Muslims accept Jesus as Savior and Lord.* They quoted Henry Martyn, the nineteenth century missionary, who spent four hours in prayer every day and could still say, *"I never expect to see a Muslim come to Christ."*

Now I ask you: Who would have the audacity, the cruelty, to stand up and question the methods of this veteran missionary couple? They have given their entire working lives to the promotion of the Gospel. They have sacrificed wealth and comfort to preach Christ. Who among the congregations they visited would dare to suggest their approach should have been altered and the results enlarged?

And yet in the mid-'60s that was exactly the question Westerners needed to confront. Remarkably few Christians faced up to it.

Bob Pierce was one of the exceptions. Deployed to China in 1947 by American Youth For Christ, Bob Pierce planned to present Premier Chiang Kai-shek with a copy of the Bible and assure him that many of America's young Christians were praying for him and his government. When Pierce arrived in Shanghai, he briefed the missionaries on his plan. Some smiled patronizingly. Others took him aside and said, *"You can't get to Generalissimo Chiang. It's impossible. We've been here thirty years, and we've never even seen him."*

"You know, John," Bob told me later. *"J. Hudson Taylor came to China. He walked down this road. Then he turned right and walked down that road. Then he turned right again, and again, and arrived back where he'd started from. A lot of these God-fearing missionaries followed the same route. They started walking around the same square. Soon the path became a rut. Then it became a ditch. Then a trench. In the*

PHIL and MARILYN GORDON. It was largely thanks to the skill and generosity of men like Phil Gordon and E. Harold Keown, Sr., that the ministry remained afloat in the 1960s.

end, *their efforts to follow J. Hudson Taylor had worn the ground so low that they couldn't see China any more."*

Only heaven will reveal how much Bob Pierce supported those missionaries through prayer, encouragement, and personal finance. But he saw clearly what happened when those in missions cannot "sacrifice their thoughts."

I asked Bob Pierce what he did to reach Chiang Kai-shek.

He told me the first thing he did was place a little distance between himself and the missionaries.

"Rather than let my thinking be neutralized by such negative thoughts," he said, *"I decided to move out of the missionary compound and check into a local hotel. I laid out my strategy without the counsel of those who thought it couldn't be done. In fact I never did see the Generalissimo on that trip – that came later. But I did see Madam Chiang Kai-shek. And through her support I was able to begin meaningful work among the people of China."*

Bob Pierce's efforts eventuated in the establishment of World Vision's orphanage program – a multi-continental, multifaceted ministry of mercy, unequaled anywhere in the world. It was a triumph – and it happened only because Bob Pierce refused to allow self-imposed limitations to paralyze creative and positive action.

So I returned from the Middle East a changed man. I was also convinced that I must distance myself a little from the conventional thinking of American missions, and start thinking outside the box. A change had begun. ∎

RALPH DOUDERA. This soft-spoken financial wizard practices a quiet stewardship that influences thousands around the globe.

Alex Ribeiro BRAZIL

Alex Dias Ribeiro, the title-winning Brazilian race car driver famous for the 'Jesus Saves' emblazoned on his cars, leads a ministry called "Athletes of Christ." It's given him a platform from which to reach tens of thousands of young sports people. The group grew from five to 150 in its first year. But the membership really began to soar after Alex returned from Haggai Institute training in Singapore in 1986. It now exceeds 4,500.

"The final paper I did for my H.I. training ended up being the very strategy we used to grow Athletes of Christ, which boosted the ministry like nothing before. Haggai Institute's focus on training leaders to train others has been heavily applied here. As a result, our leaders are multiplying."

He's also learned to communicate more effectively. *"The communication techniques I learned at H.I. completely changed my approach to reaching others. I've started focusing on the receiver of the message instead of the sender. For example I've changed the entire writing style of a publication we produce that goes out to 35,000 soccer players."*

Leaders trained by Ribeiro since his return home from Haggai Institute number in the hundreds. Says Ribeiro, *"I knew where I wanted to go before my H.I. training, but I didn't know how to get there. I came back from H.I. with a new strategy, ready to set goals, organize my time better, and lead and train people with greater effectiveness. I am a good example of how H.I. training really works."*

15

3 Steep Ascent

HANK BRONSON. In 1985 Hank and Dottie Bronson gave a million dollars for a potential H.I. base on Oahu. It was the profit on the resale of that property that God used to launch the current H.I. training center on Maui.

It was around this time the trustees suggested we change the name of the crusade ministry to Evangelism International, since more and more time was being allocated to work outside the United States. I liked the term. It wasn't until we mounted a crusade in Jakarta in 1968, though, that an answer to the missions problem began to take shape.

That campaign, which took several months to set up, owed much to the persistence of Dr. Gerald F. Beavan and my associate James Frame. Never before in the history of Indonesia had the two largest Church groups, the Pentecostals and the Presbyterians, actually cooperated on a missions venture. They had asked me to bring a group of evangelists – ordained and lay – for an event that would climax in Jakarta's Senajan Stadium, Indonesia's largest. I recruited a group of fifty-six men and women, and had them flown to Seattle, where I'd scheduled to join them for the flight to Jakarta. On the night before my early morning departure, I received a cablegram from a prominent Indonesian leader. The words jumped off the page:

Do not bring group to Indonesia. You will be denied entry. Should you get through Customs, you will be denied hotel rooms. Repeat: do not come.

I'd known that the recent spiritual awakening in Indonesia had heightened tension between the country's Christian and Muslim populations. But the cancellation of the trip was an outcome I hadn't even dreamed of. The group had invested over $145,000 in the crusade – and back in 1968 that was a lot of money. These busy professionals – doctors, businessmen, clergy – had wrenched their schedules to join me. They were already in transit. The collapse of the venture at this point would destroy my credibility and torpedo my ministry.

I prayed fervently. But I admit I was on tenterhooks. At about two in the morning I went to the refrigerator to pour a glass of milk. I didn't even like milk – that's how stressed out I was. Opening the refrigerator door I thought to myself, *"Aren't you the guy who wrote the book* How to Win over Worry? *Look at you. You're in shambles."* And from that point I left the matter in the hands of God and went to sleep.

Next morning I was awakened by a call from Western Union. *"Ignore previous cable,"* read the operator. *"God is on the throne. Anticipating arrival of you and your group."*

I showered, closed my suitcase, and rushed to the airport. Thankfully, no one knew what had happened – or so I thought. That evening during the briefing, one of the team put his hand up.

"Someone told me we're not going to be allowed into Indonesia," he said. *"What shall we do? Isn't this a terrible risk we're taking, and a terrible gamble with funds?"*

I was astounded this man had obtained the information. Just as I was thinking how to phrase my reply, however, Dr. Clarence Sands, pastor of the great San Jose First Baptist Church, and dean of California Bay Area Ministers, said, *"Yeah, I heard the same thing from the same blabbermouth. We can't gauge our actions or determine our plans on irresponsible mouthings like that."*

The team going to Indonesia. Many of those in the picture became the founding members of Haggai Institute.

That was all that needed to be said. We went through the Indonesian immigration and customs without a hitch, and enjoyed the finest accommodation in what was at that time the only air-conditioned hotel in equatorial West Java. But our problems were not over.

"We realize Dr. Haggai may be shot tonight…"

The first cable, it turned out, reflected divisions among Indonesia's Christian leadership. Soon after we arrived, one of the leaders asked me, *"How can you live with your conscience, when you know that communicating the Gospel of Jesus Christ could so antagonize the Muslims? Are you aware that the Muslims burned twenty-nine Churches in the Sulawesi Islands just a few weeks ago?"*

It was a heartfelt objection. But I knew we'd never get anywhere if we predicated our whole approach to evangelism on fear of reprisals. Also, I knew Indonesia was keen to participate in the world market. I conjectured that this alone would induce the government to provide protection to non-Muslim visitors. I voiced these thoughts to the leader. And don't forget, I added, one of the five pillars of the Indonesian Pancasila is *freedom of religion*.

Tensions like this underlaid the whole crusade. A day before the meetings at Senajan Stadium the government had still not given us final approval, and a crowd of students had set up a demonstration outside. Ostensibly this was about recent increases in the price of rice – but Indonesians knew what was really behind it. The students didn't want a Christian meeting in the stadium, and they were making sure it didn't happen.

What followed remains to this day one of my most unforgettable answers to prayer. We had

MARGE LINDSEY. Not only has this remarkable lady given into the eight figures, she has also made several world trips for H.I. and maintained an unparalleled writing schedule to encourage H.I. personnel.

scheduled the crusade for the middle of the dry season – not realizing that good weather for crusades meant also good weather for demonstrators. And yet on each day of the meetings it rained so hard that the students had to run for cover. Then at 5:00 p.m. the rain cleared, leaving us to proceed on schedule with the meeting at 6:30 p.m. People came out in droves. Before our first meeting, I met with the local committee just before the service began. Our chairman, John DeFretes, stood up and prayed in a loud voice, *"Oh Lord, we thank you for bringing Dr. Haggai all the way across the waters to be with us. We know he is in Your hands. We realize he may be shot tonight, but we rest in Thy will."*

It was then I learned the real meaning of the phrase *"Watch and pray."* I prayed with one eye closed and watched with the other. When the praying finished, another committee member – in a gesture to console me – leaned over and said, *"Don't worry, Brother Haggai, there are 250 plainclothes policemen in the stadium."* I did a quick calculation. That meant one plainclothes policeman to every 32 people – not a great comfort. Out there on the platform I'd be a sitting duck for terrorists.

Fortunately I didn't get shot. The meeting went off smoothly, and that night hundreds accepted Christ as their personal Savior.

But in one way, the difficulties we'd faced only illustrated the wider problem for foreigners doing evangelism. Much as I enjoyed conducting crusades, I knew it was well past time for local Church leaders to take full responsibility for evangelism in their own cultures. In fact many leaders during that crusade took me aside and questioned me about my methods as an evangelist. So many that I was obliged to hold a brief seminar on the "how" of evangelism.

That seminar planted the seed from which Haggai Institute grew. In a culture of nationalism,

EDDIE LIEBERMAN. Founding trustee, Bible scholar, communicator, mentor and friend. Eddie Lieberman is the only man I know who consistently receives standing ovations for his lectures at Haggai Institute.

19

DAVID WONG. Scholar, author, and pastor for 20 years of a rapidly growing and extremely fruitful Presbyterian church in Singapore, David Wong served as Director of Training in Maui from 1994 to 2001, when he became Vice President, International Training.

Dr. Justin Harris, an Indian Methodist leader from Mumbai, told me that *"What the non-Western Church needs from the West is training. The rest – the evangelism itself – we can do far better than any missionary, because we are preaching to people whose language and culture we share."*

Hammering the iron

The late Cecil B. Day, Sr., founder and chairman of the Day's Inn motel chain, became one of Haggai Institute's earliest and foremost supporters.

He later told me the motel idea had come to him at two o'clock in the morning. He got out of bed, grabbed a yellow legal pad, and wrote for fourteen hours until he had the blueprint for the Day's Inn motel. He said God alone had opened his mind to the possibility of the budget luxury motel. There were no committees or consultations. The idea for the "Volkswagen of motels" came to him in solitude.

Over the months following Jakarta, I spent a good deal of time listening to the counsel of others – particularly Bob Pierce, my brother Tom Haggai, and Jerry Beavan. But like Cecil Day, I also spent time on my own, thrashing out the principles that remain basic to the Haggai Institute approach.

As I saw it, world missions required leadership, but not leadership for leadership's sake – rather, leadership for evangelism's sake. I had no desire to replace preaching missionaries with teaching missionaries. To be effective, the whole venture must rest on different foundations. In the privacy of the Bali Beach Hotel in Indonesia, I reduced my philosophy of world evangelism to seven basics:

1.   Training should focus on Christians whose leadership had already been demonstrated in the Church and in the professions.

2. Training for such leaders in the developing world should be provided by faculty from the developing world, using materials written in the developing world.

3. Training should be provided in time-frames short enough that busy and influential people could realistically fit it into their schedules.

4. Training should as far as possible take place in a neutral location, and certainly not in Western countries from which participants would return to be branded "Uncle Toms."

5. Training should be replicable – in fact participants should be selected for sessions only if they agree to pass the training on once they return to their home nations.

6. Training should not be funded exclusively from the United States. Rather, to increase the perceived value of the seminars and prevent dependence on Western donors, each participant should be asked to bear part of the cost.

7. Training should be conducted in English – simply because after World War II, English had become the language of choice for most of the world's people.

Dr. ANTHONY D'SOUZA. Founder and director of the Xavier Institute of Leadership in Mumbai, India, and a former consultant to the UN, Dr. D'Souza brings style and depth of insight to his H.I. lectures.

Between principle and praxis lies a hard road, as anyone knows who has tried to get a fresh concept off the ground. Though God had given me the confidence of Christian leaders – particularly in Asia – who wanted this type of training, I needed also the trust and support of visionaries with the financial muscle to back it. This took years longer than I had expected, but the passionate desire of the Asian

21

leaders compelled me to persevere. And for the glory of God, I was determined to put the philosophy into action.

The program takes its bow

After a great deal of work and many heart-rending setbacks, we scheduled the first international seminar for 15 September to 24 October 1969. Participants came from four developing countries to a lovely facility on Lake Brienz in German-speaking Switzerland. Switzerland seemed the obvious place for such a program. After all, wasn't the name Switzerland synonymous with neutrality and internationalism? And wasn't it also the chosen headquarters of the international YMCA and the International Red Cross? The five-week session would cost around $100,000. Only one problem persisted: we had no money.

In the spring of that year, 1969, I'd had reason to believe the money would be in hand. I'd thoroughly counted on a $50,000 gift from an international oil tycoon. The owner of the largest private trucking company in America had committed $20,000. Other smaller gifts had been coming in, and everything looked on track.

But at two in the afternoon on September 9, my secretary Alberta Shuler came in with a message from Pan American Airlines. If we didn't get the money to them by the following morning, she said, I would have to cancel the trip. Then she paused and added, *"Dr. Haggai, why does God permit things like this?"*

I understood the question. But I also knew that if things were going wrong it was my fault, not God's. Perhaps in my enthusiasm for the program I'd misunderstood the leading of the Lord. I knew I needed to spend time in prayer, and turned to go

BOB and CHERRY RUTLAND. Majordomo of a billion-dollar auto-hauling industry, Bob Rutland helped pay off the mortgage on Maui. He and Cherry have made several world trips with H.I. At the time of writing, Bob serves as the Chairman of Haggai Institute's International Board of Trustees (2002-2004).

into my office. Before closing the door, I directed my secretary, *"Please take down this cablegram message. Due to unexpected and unavoidable obstacles, training session postponed indefinitely. Regrets, regards, prayers, Haggai."* Then, for reasons I still don't know, I added, *"Don't send this until four o'clock. If you don't hear from me by then, send it out."*

I went into my office and closed the door. I spread-eagled myself face-down on the carpet, asking God to show me how to salvage what could be salvaged and minimize the reproach to His name. I asked Him to forgive me where I had gone ahead of Him. I prayed without stopping for one and three-quarter hours. And then my secretary's voice came over the intercom.

"Yes? What is it?" I barked, with a strain in my voice that showed my impatience.

"Carl Newton of San Antonio is on the line."

"I'm sorry, I can't talk to him now. I'll call him back," I said.

*"But you **must** talk to him,"* she insisted.

"I don't have to talk with anyone right now," I said. *"Not even the Archangel Gabriel. I'm talking to his Boss."*

But she persisted. Although I was annoyed at her, I took the call.

"Hi, Carl. How can I help you?"

"John," he said, *"the market has gone to pot. My stock has dropped from $57 a share to $13 a share since May."*

I'd been straining my ears all day for encouraging news like that!

"I'm sorry, Carl," I replied. *"I've been talking to the Lord about another matter, and I'll include the problem in my prayers."*

"Wait a minute, knucklehead," he cut in. *"You need some money, don't you?"*

"Of course. But you don't sound as if you're in a position to help."

CECIL and DEEN DAY.
In 1971 Cecil Day grasped the concept and implications of H.I.'s work with astounding speed. Thousands of H.I. graduates trained in the Day Center he funded in Singapore and his widow Deen has remained a generous supporter of the ministry.

MARY ANNA FOWLER.
A successful businesswoman,
Mary Anna Fowler first
became acquainted with
Haggai Institute in 1978.
She came onto the board
in 1990 and now serves on
the Executive Committee.

"Well, John, I can't give you any stock. Since I'm CEO and a major stockholder, the divestiture of any of my stock could cause a run on the company."

"I understand, Carl."

"But wait a minute. We're able to get an eight percent, $100,000 loan for twelve months. Within this time I should be able to arrange for some liquidity. Call the man at your bank in Atlanta. Janie and I wired a gift of $100,000 a couple of hours ago."

I could scarcely believe my ears. When I hung up the phone, the clock on my desk said six minutes to four. Ten minutes later, there would have been no training session, and probably no Haggai Institute.

Later, Carl told me, *"I didn't know how I was going to do it, but I was impelled to act. It's a strange thing. I've never made a commitment I was proud of, which at the time I could see any possibility of fulfilling."* It's an extraordinary claim – but one that many among our donors will endorse.

Measured on any scale, that first session was enormously blessed by God. After that, the ministry went from strength to strength. A participant at the second session – Roland J. Payne, holder of two academic doctorates and Bishop of the Lutheran Church in Liberia – told me later, *"I will never forget the ministry and witness we encountered in Switzerland. What you started here should have been started twenty years ago."*

That said it all. ■

Vichai Trangkhasombat THAILAND

Throughout the churches of Thailand, Vichai Trangkhasombat is affectionately known as Mr. Coca-Cola.

Rescued from bombardment in Saigon and later from imminent bankruptcy, Vichai renounced Buddhism and accepted Jesus as Lord. It was his transfer to Hong Kong as a top executive with Coca-Cola that brought him in contact with Haggai Institute. Attending a seminar changed his life.

"I learned a great deal from the other participants. I also discovered, through the H.I vision for reaching the world for Christ, how Asian Christian leaders and businessmen like myself are qualified to help evangelize Asia."

One thing Vichai did soon after returning to Thailand was to set up 34 financial foundations to support the work of poor churches. In 1991 he founded the Fellowship of Serving the Ministry for Business and Professional Men and Women, to bring people from the business community into local congregations.

"Before I attended the H.I. seminar," he says, *"I thought I was really an effective Christian. But when I returned home, I was more than ever committed to bringing Christ to my people – to reaching my country for the living God."*

25

4 The Road to Singapore

BILL HINSON. Two years before the first training session, Dr. William M. Hinson was supporting the H.I. program. He later led his church, the prestigious First Baptist of Fort Lauderdale, Florida, to make a generous monthly gift to H.I.

A gifted speaker and brilliant administrator, he personifies H.I.'s commitment to the "permanence factor" in relationships. As the first president to serve H.I. after my appointment to chairman, he has given sterling leadership during a period of transition and rapid growth. He now serves as CEO and vice chairman.

So the concept worked. We held another training session the following year. Very quickly the new ministry needed people to oversee its operation and expansion.

From the outset, Dr. Ernest Watson grasped the concept. I'd heard of him almost fifteen years earlier. Dr. Watson had pastored some influential Churches in Australia and was a pioneer of religious radio and television broadcasting. His birth to British parents could have marked him as a white Westerner, but his rearing and ministry placed him squarely in the East. As one international leader commented, *"He's a Baptist, but he's bigger than any denomination. He's an Australian, but his influence extends around the world."*

Dr. Watson served as Dean from the very first session. At this point Dr. Watson was sixty-five years of age. At normal retirement age, he put his considerable reputation on the line to identify himself with an untried, highly criticized mission concept. For six years Dr. Watson held those seminars together, with the collaboration of such stellar world Christian leaders as Dr. Han of Korea, Dr. Accad of Beruit, Lebanon, and Dr. Max Atienza of Manila, Philippines. His selfless devotion both to the command of Christ and to the highest welfare of the developing world was a major factor in establishing the ministry.

Where should the ministry live?

Having held the first seminars in Switzerland, our first instinct was to stay there. Before the first seminar, in late 1968, a colleague had introduced me to his father, who owned a hotel in the French-speaking sector of Switzerland and had long dreamed of using the facility for training evangelists. It seemed a plain blessing from God.

It wasn't. We were all set to finalize the purchase when, with just twelve hours to go, we had to scuttle our plans. We'd learned that loans on the property amounted to more than the sale price – in other words, we'd have been strapped with the intolerable burden of paying off twice the value of the property. By then we'd already hired an architect from London to suggest improvements, and the forced reversal cost us hundreds of hours and thousands of dollars.

Still we clung to the notion of Switzerland. Just a year later, Dr. Bob Pierce told me of a property in German-speaking Switzerland, near the site of the first seminar on Lake Brienz. A former missionary had built this three-story chalet. He'd run out of money. We agreed on a sale price of $300,000. Shortly after we'd paid him the first $100,000, the owner reneged on commitments over his signature – a move that caused his own lawyer to abandon him. The trustees knew we had an open-and-shut case and were planning to institute litigation to recover the money. But the saintly Dr. Han Kyung Chik of Seoul, Korea, said to me in soft tones I shall never forget, *"Dr. Haggai, even though you may be right, if you were to go to court in this matter, it would bring an end to your ministry in Asia."*

We had to walk away from the loss. And I had to go back to Carl Newton, who'd given much of the money, and tell him what had happened.

With a smile, Carl said, *"I think I need to hire you in my company. I just lost two million dollars in Mexico!"*

What a great spirit!

In retrospect, the whole thinking that favored Switzerland as a location was misdirected – for a number of reasons:

AUDREY and RICHARD BOWIE. Audrey Bowie's lectures at H.I. women's sessions have been a powerful influence on women in developing nations. Her husband Richard, formerly principal of Bishop's Anglican Theological College in Calcutta, has played a major role in the implementation and oversight of the H.I. training program.

1. At this period hijackings were common. Not surprisingly, then, leaders from the East didn't savor the prospect of a flight refueling in Middle Eastern capitals where hijackings were most likely to occur.

2. Both the climate and the cuisine were unfamiliar to most participants – crucially, for Eastern participants, Swiss meals seldom included rice.

3. Though all the leaders coming to the sessions spoke English, few spoke German. So if any difficulties arose with airline connections, it was hard for them to contact us. Most didn't even know enough German to ask for an English-speaking telephone operator.

4. The facility we used in Switzerland was two and a half hours from the airport in Zurich, so picking people up and getting them back turned into a logistical nightmare.

5. Last – and by no means least from the fundraising viewpoint – Switzerland simply sent the wrong message. Talk about Switzerland and most people think of numbered bank accounts and expensive ski holidays – they don't think about Christian leaders from developing countries in need of crucial training. Basing the ministry in Switzerland, therefore, made fund-raising harder work.

HAN KYUNG CHIK. Though pastor emeritus of the world's largest Presbyterian church in Seoul, Korea, Dr. Han still carved out time to serve as H.I.'s senior faculty member.

I remember talking to my son Johnny about the ministry – as I did often. *"I guess Switzerland's the most beautiful place on the face of the earth,"* I said. *"But it really bothers me. It would be better if we could conduct our sessions in the developing world itself. There are too many examples of nationals trained in the West who become spoiled by Western thinking and cannot effectively relate to their own people."*

Johnny agreed. Out of such considerations came the crucial decision in 1971 to base the ministry in Singapore. Politically, Singapore remains as neutral as Switzerland. It stands at the crossroads of the Orient, within 3,000 miles of half the world's population. Its climate and cuisine are more compatible with the needs of Eastern participants. It has a good racial mix, in addition to which over eighty-five percent of the population speak English. It's clean, orderly, uncorrupt, and being only 230 square miles in extent has no location in its territories more than thirty minutes away from the international airport.

Singapore was the ideal location. It's just unfortunate that we transferred our operations there a few weeks before President Nixon floated the dollar.

And the dollar goes down...

For years, I had been circumnavigating the world three, four, and sometimes five times a year. The pressure mounted as I put in place a self-imposed limit never to be away from home more than three weeks at a stretch. I would fly at night, and on arrival in the morning would negotiate with the hotel for a room. I asked them, *"What is your best rate?"* At that time it was about 18 dollars. I said *"I'd like to rent a room for two hours, and I'll give you $2 an hour."* If they objected, I'd follow up, *"You've got the room. It will help you pay for your maid service and other peripheral costs, and you'll make a very happy customer out of me, and in years to come I may bring you a lot of business."*

I cannot remember one time that I failed to get the room. After a bath I'd lay my clothes out, then flop across the bed and sleep soundly until the

BOB GLAZE. A Dallas businessman/developer, he was a major force in the acquisition of the initial properties in both Singapore and Maui. He served Haggai Institute as treasurer from 1986 to 1994.

telephone operator gave me a wake-up call. As I fell into bed I'd hope and pray that they wouldn't throw me out before time. They never did, and since that time these same hotels have made a handsome profit on their investment.

Another cost-cutting device: I'd arrange to fly on Pan Am, which arrived in Tokyo at 7 o'clock. The last flight of the day left Tokyo for Hong Kong at the same time, which obliged Pan Am to put me up at the Keio Plaza Hotel. I'd then arrange to see my Japanese contacts from late evening till 2 a.m., squeezing in another meeting before my flight left next day. The contacts were essential. But the travel was expensive, and every economy helped.

Meanwhile, as I raced around the world trying to secure a future for the ministry, Johnny's condition grew progressively worse. Tensions inevitably emerged. My wife Christine urged me to cut down on the travel, partly for my health, and partly so I could spend more time with my son. The periods of separation pained us all. I knew Chris was carrying a terrific burden. But even when I was home, I couldn't escape from the program's demands. At a social occasion with family, she knew my mind was on the next action I needed to take to keep the ministry afloat.

I'd told her in 1970 – and I really believed it – that within twelve months the ministry would be in good enough shape that I could cut down my frenetic schedule. In one of those heart-to-heart conversations, I told her, *"Honey, God has made sensitive to this work some of the people whose gifts will help alleviate the pressure. I really believe I'll be able to reduce my work load twenty percent by the end of the year."*

Next August, just after we'd committed to Singapore, Richard Nixon cut the dollar loose from the Gold Standard and let it float. The effect was equivalent to rapid devaluation. On the morning

In years of almost continuous travel, just occasionally CHRIS and I had the pleasure of traveling together.

of August 15, one American dollar would buy 3.33 Singapore dollars. Within four short months it would buy only 2.40. The result: to maintain commitments in Singapore we needed almost double the funds. We were in deep financial trouble. Far from easing off, I realized that for the next eighteen months I'd be working harder than I'd ever worked in my life.

I called Jim Frame, a Dallas businessman who was then my associate and later joined the Haggai Institute board. *"Jim,"* I said, *"give me the name of somebody here in Atlanta who has money, will admit it, can make a decision, and can make it instantly. I want somebody who is not going to blow a lot of smoke like telling me he's got to pray about if for thirty days, or discuss it with his family, or wait for his board to meet. Tell me somebody who can make a decision now."*

Jim Frame's response was unhesitating: *"Cecil Day."*

That stumped me. *"Who in the world is Cecil Day?"* I asked him.

"He's the guy building that budget-luxury motel at Clairmont and I-85."

I got on the telephone and was put through to him.

"Mr. Day," I said, *"I know you're a busy man, and so am I. So I'm not going to take a lot of your time. In order to get to the point quickly, I'd like to come over to see you right now. I have an important matter. I'll walk out of your office in exactly ten minutes by the clock."*

"What do you want to see me about?" he asked.

"Money."

"How much?"

"Oh come on, Mr. Day," I said. *"You know that no one gives away interview information when he's setting up an appointment."*

He chuckled.

CRAIG and **EMILIE WIERDA.** God used this remarkable couple to reach key players in America's Dutch community. With businesses in automobiles, aircraft leasing and investment, they have given in the seven figures and maintain personal contact with H.I. principals all over the world.

"But I'll tell you this," I added. *"I'm bringing some smelling salts in my left hand and some camphor in my right hand to revive you when you hear how much I'm asking for."*

Cecil Day invited me over. This time, though, I was the one to be surprised. When I walked into Day's office, a tall, handsome thirty-five-year-old flashed a smile and said, *"You don't remember me, do you?"*

Now if there's one thing that crushes the morale of a fundraiser it's realizing how badly he's prepared himself.

"No," I replied. *"I'm embarrassed. I really don't."*

Cecil Day reminded me that seven years earlier I'd conducted a meeting at the Mount Vernon Baptist Church of Atlanta.

"I was amazed that you had offered a hundred dollar, hand-tooled family Bible to the person who would bring the largest number of people to the concluding Sunday night service. You told them that the number they brought had to be over the qualifying number of twenty-five. I was surprised first of all that you could get by with that in a Church like Mount Vernon. And I was intrigued that you put a floor of twenty-five under the challenge."

I laughed. *"When you have studied the heroic proportions of my profile,"* I said, *"you'll know that I'm not about to give a hundred-dollar, hand-tooled Bible to someone who brings only his next-door neighbor."*

Cecil reminded me that his brother, Lon, had won the Bible by bringing forty-two people. Among those forty-two were Cecil, his wife Deen, and his five children. Then it all came back to me, and I remembered the entire episode.

Cecil asked, *"So how much do you want?"*

"Thirty-four thousand, seven hundred dollars," I said. *"Will you write out a check, please?"*

"No, I won't."

I looked at my watch, then looked at him

With Canon Yɪᴘ Tᴜɴɢ Sʜᴀɴ. A Singapore shipping magnate who entered the Anglican priesthood in later life, Canon Yip has shown consummate skill and inspiration as chairman of the Singapore board.

and said, *"Well, you have just saved yourself seven minutes. Thank you for seeing me. I've got to go."*

"Where are you going?" he asked.

"To raise that thirty-four thousand, seven hundred dollars."

"I'll give you five thousand dollars. But I won't give it to you all at once. I'll write you four post-dated checks for one thousand, two hundred and fifty dollars each. Will that do it?"

"No," I said, *"it won't. But it will help. Especially if you make a photocopy of the checks."*

He looked nonplussed.

"It's predicated on a sound biblical principle," I told him. *"Provoke one another to good works. I want others to see what you've done. It may get their minds out of the hundred-dollar range."*

Cecil Day agreed to my proposal. And that was the beginning of one of the most incredible odysseys of stewardship that I've had the privilege to observe. From that initial gift came office space in his new building, the donation of what became the Day Center in Singapore, and other gifts of enormous size.

A ministry of the East

By God's grace, we managed to ride the fall of the dollar. Securing property was still a challenge, however, and in 1971, I had the strongest impression I should go to Singapore. I couldn't articulate the reason – I simply knew I had to go. I called some of my trustees and asked what they thought. They said, *"If the Lord is guiding you, you must do it."*

Though I didn't mention it, the problem was money. Nobody offered to buy my ticket, so I went to the bank, raised a loan, and flew to Singapore. Within hours after arriving, a Singapore Chinese friend introduced me to a young lawyer by the name of Lai Kew Chai. We got to talking about property.

Justice **LAI KEW CHAI**. **As a young solicitor, Lai Kew Chai played a crucial role in securing Haggai Institute's establishment as a Singapore corporation. He has remained a stalwart friend and board member of the ministry.**

This 31-year-old Malaysian-born, Chinese Singaporean barrister, who would later become the respected Mr. Justice Lai Kew Chai of the High Court in Singapore, listened attentively and immediately identified the action we needed to take. Within hours he had initiated the process to make the ministry a Singapore corporation.

In less than thirty hours, I was on a plane back to the United States. Haggai Institute (as it had by now become) was incorporated as Haggai Institute for Advanced Leadership Training Ltd. Thenceforth it was a Singaporean corporation under the Singapore Companies Act, with a local board of directors led ably by Canon Yip Tung Shan – a shipping magnate who'd entered the Anglican priesthood, and father-in-law to Lai Kew Chai.

Karel Sinaga INDONESIA

Karel Sinaga is a major player in the Indonesian insurance market. His company Bumi Asih Jaya is the seventh largest of Indonesia's 65 insurance firms.

The name literally means: "Where you find love, the place will prosper." Says Sinaga, "My aim is not just to make this company big and great. That's good, but it's not the first thing. Whether my company grows to 5,000 or 10,000 employees, I want to lead all of them to the Lord. That is my goal."

In 1998 Karel Sinaga became Haggai Institute's first Asian chairman of the International Board of Trustees. He credits H.I. with changing his whole perspective about being a Christian businessman and leader.

"I realized that the training which was so beneficial to me would be beneficial to others as well. So I began to teach people here what I learned at Haggai Institute. I would like to see more Christian leaders attend seminars. We have to do our utmost to equip godly leaders for evangelism."

Over the years, I have received enormous support from these quiet Singapore leaders. And to my dying day, I will applaud the expansiveness of spirit that gave the American board the grace to release a measure of control. It was an act of humility conspicuously absent among the mission groups active in Beirut on my visit of 1964. The board members were willing to support what they could not dominate.

Such was the demand for Haggai Institute's program, however, that within ten years it was clear the flagship facility in Singapore simply could not accommodate enough leaders or sessions. A second center was critically needed.

Over the Andes – and beyond

Another factor came into play here. Haggai Institute began its work on the Pacific Rim, and with good reason. For one thing, Asia had – and still has – the lion's share of the world's population. For another, large blocks of it were closed to traditional Western missions and to that extent were deprived of that kind of Gospel witness.

By a remarkable chain of events, however, we'd already found our focus widened. Dr. Bill Hinson was the first Baptist pastor to include Haggai Institute in his congregational budget. It was through Bill and his wife Bettye that I met Tom Cundy, and in turn through Tom Cundy that I met representatives of the Maclellan Foundation of Chattanooga, Tennessee. Without that link, the Foundation's president, Hugh O. Maclellan, would never have been able to introduce me to the Presbyterian missionary to Brazil Bill Mosely, and the Brazilian Christian statesman Dr. Benjamin Moraes.

These two men – Mosely and Moraes – were instrumental in bringing our attention to the needs

A second center was critically needed.

of Latin America. Until then I hadn't considered Latin America a priority. After all, Latin Americans had the Bible, while most Asians did not. A few months later, though, when I arrived in Singapore for a session, Dr. Watson told me, *"Dr. Moraes is in Japan, and he's taking an eight-hour flight here just to talk with you about including Latin America in the Haggai Institute program."*

I met him the next day. I found him charming and persuasive. Dr. Moraes could read, write and speak twelve languages. He'd written the penal code for Brazil and served as a cabinet minister on three different occasions. He'd built the Copacabana Presbyterian Church into a world-renowned Church, written forty books, and currently taught law at the University of Rio de Janeiro.

"You must understand," he said, *"that the Gospel of Jesus Christ is not reaching the cross-section of Brazilians. We thank God for the missionaries, but they are either working with Indians in the mountains, doing translation work, or pursuing some vocational activity in the cities. No one is doing for Brazil what Haggai Institute is doing for Asia."*

The Haggai Institute board endorsed this appeal. As the first Brazilian participant, Dr. Moraes sent the Rev. Guilhermino Cunha, senior associate minister of the Copacabana Church. And from there the work of Haggai Institute in Latin America mushroomed.

Expansion into Latin America made the need for another training center even more urgent. The numbers waiting for training already exceeded our capacity in Singapore. An additional facility would relieve the pressure. The question was: *Where should*

Fort Canning Lodge, Haggai Institute's flagship training facility in Singapore. It remains foundational to H.I.'s global program of leadership training.

"Singapore 2" be launched? Asian leaders encouraged the selection of Hawaii. Though part of the United States, they insisted, it was only 22 percent Caucasian and not generally identified as Western. It would significantly reduce travel time and costs. And that would mean more graduates trained at a reduced overhead, allowing more people to be reached with the Good News of the Gospel.

In fact, the final location turned out to be the island of Maui. The first training sessions began there in 1993. The venue we leased – the $28 million, 229-room Maui Sun Hotel – was ideally located just 20 minutes from the airport. Shortly before that time a Japanese business group had offered $62 million for the property. But before the contract was settled the Japanese bubble burst, and when the Maui Sun went into receivership Haggai Institute was able to purchase it for just $13 million.

Haggai Institute's Mid-Pacific Center on Maui. University presidents, leading pastors, supreme court judges, government officials and top professionals meet here to advance their skills in leadership for evangelism.

The new building met our expanded training needs and assured adequate space well into the future. Six acres of attractively landscaped grounds provide an atmosphere conducive to prayerful reflection. The interior space accommodates teaching and small-group work, and encourages a high level of interaction among participants. In the two 6-story towers the mix of single unit rooms, small suites and guest quarters make the facility ideal for participants, faculty and friends of Haggai Institute who want to see the ministry up close. ■

Joaquina Pajaro
THE PHILIPPINES

"I was shy, lazy, and indifferent to God's work – until I went to Haggai Institute," says Joaquina Pajaro, a retired professor of mathematics in Manila.

Mrs. Pajaro (left) shown with another H.I. alumna, Mrs. Rex Reyes, found the training sessions in Singapore so intense that she nearly gave up. She realized, though, that despite generous giving she'd stayed on the sidelines of Christian work. In the second week of the seminar she knelt by her bed and prayed, *"Lord, as of now I'm committing my life to serve you."*

When she returned home to the Philippines, her friends were amazed at the 'new' Joaquina. Her husband Eliseo said, *"She was an entirely different person. I couldn't believe it!"*

Within a month, Joaquina had organized her first training seminar, and for two years spearheaded evangelistic campaigns inside and outside her church. She became a catalyst for outreach at a women's prison, and was later elected chairwoman for the united Methodist Commission on Mission for the West Metro Manila district, initiating a vigorous program of church-planting.

None of this would have happened had Joaquina not attended a seminar at Haggai Institute. *"If it were not for the H.I. training,"* she says, *"I wouldn't know what to do. The training has giving me a better understanding of evangelism and follow-up. It had impressed upon me that we need to take the Gospel to others."*

5 Haggai Institute Now

I'm sometimes asked why in 1974 Evangelism International changed its name to Haggai Institute. After all, on the face of it there seems no particular reason to give the organization the name of its founder. Isn't it just an ego-trip?

Well here's the reason. Within two years of naming the crusade ministry Evangelism International in 1962, no less than four other organizations had taken the same name. This led to difficulties. When a lady in Greenville, Texas, left a bequest of $5,000 to "Evangelism International," it cost us more than the $5,000 to prove that we were the intended ministry. Her family had no doubts about this and were totally supportive – the opposition came from the other organizations of the same name, who quite innocently supposed she'd left the money to them.

So the matter of the name again came up for discussion.

The trustees said, *"Doesn't your name in Arabic mean 'pilgrim'?"*

I said, *"Yes. It's a name given to anyone who goes to Mecca three times. It is also given to a Christian who goes to the Holy Sepulcher on at least three pilgrimages. My forebear had made seven pilgrimages to Jerusalem in the 1820s, back in the day when the 150-mile distance required the better part of a week to travel."*

"Why don't we call it Haggai Institute?" someone said. *"Surely no one's going to pirate that name."*

So we did – and they haven't.

PAUL J. and JANE MEYER. In their morning devotions, Paul and Jane pray for H.I. before they pray for anything else. Our first-ever million-dollar-a-year giver, Paul established and underwrote H.I.'s development department.

Discretion the byword

The choice of name had a crucial – if unforeseen – effect.

When Idi Amin was on the loose in Uganda, an anesthesiologist called Dr. Kityo came to Singapore for the advanced leadership program. With misty eyes and a tremor in his voice he told me, *"Thank God your stationery makes no mention of a Church, the Bible, evangelism, or Christianity. If it had, I could have been sent to prison or been tortured and killed. The government is sensitive about intellectuals leaving the country, but since Singapore is looked on as the brain-export capital of the developing world, and I was leaving for 'advanced leadership training,' they gave me my travel documents."*

A quarter of a century later, this remains a highly sensitive point. There are many areas of the world – Islamic states being a good example – where living as a Christian is dangerous. There are others where, though Christianity is officially tolerated, approaches made by external Church agencies meet stiff resistance from the government. Working with people in such situations calls for diplomacy, carefulness, and tact. Thoughtlessness can cost lives.

Let me give an example. One American organization, blessed of God and highly effective in the West, decided to send scores of young people into the Arabic-speaking countries for the purpose of securing names and addresses. The follow-up stage of the plan was to mail an evangelistic letter, in Arabic, directly to the people contacted by the young Americans.

To traditional Western thinking, this made a lot of sense – you identified your market, then you sent out your advertising. Someone working on that program could have gone into almost any Church in America and won instant and unanimous

Pastor Zhang preaching in Xi'an, China. Because of the cultural revolution, when Christian leadership training was banned, China "lost a generation of leaders."

support. But look at it more closely. All kinds of delicate implications had simply not been thought through. For example:

1. In Islamic states, young girls soliciting names and addresses of local citizens could get into serious trouble.

2. Young men asking for names and addresses of women could get into serious trouble.

3. Very likely, an influx of letters from the United States would arouse suspicions in the postal authorities and lead to widespread confiscation of mail.

4. The addressees of evangelistic letters could be put in jeopardy by even an implied association with Western Christianity.

RALPH and HARRIET NEWTON. **With first-hand experience of medical practice in India and Africa, Ralph Newton and his wife Harriet have supported H.I. with money, prayer, encouragement, and exemplary leadership.**

Why would any Christian group put its workers, its program, and its target audience in such danger? The only answer I can think of is: *they didn't think.* And they surely didn't understand the culture. In their eagerness to serve God, these dedicated men and women failed to exercise reasonable caution or to take into account the real needs of the people they so desperately wanted to help.

In such minefields, Haggai Institute has trodden very carefully. It has been a ground rule of our operations overseas to do nothing that might be construed as interference in the affairs of a sovereign state. We do not smuggle participants out of a country any more than we smuggle Bibles in. We work openly, with the consent of the relevant authorities. We are frank about what we do. But we also exercise all necessary discretion so as not to put the leaders we work with in difficulty.

Lovely Ai-Yin Ko TAIWAN

"The Taiwanese think Christianity is a religion unrelated to their lives."

So says Lovely Ai-Yin Ko, the English instructor at Soo Chow University in Taipei. Her work gives her many opportunities to share faith with students in a country where only 3% are Christians.

"Don't expect a vacation," she laughs, recalling her time in Singapore. *"In those weeks you're going to be studying, writing, reading, and learning so much you need another year to digest it. I came back with a big notebook and was so excited because I immediately began using the materials, even in the communication classes at the university. That's the difference about Haggai Institute. You take information home to use."*

In a new venture, Lovely leads an adult Sunday school class where she passes on her Haggai Institute training. *"I want others to dream big for the Lord,"* she says.

That's why Haggai Institute doesn't send out mass mailings or advertise in the newspapers or on T.V. One way we can protect our alumni in sensitive areas is by ensuring we don't gain a high media profile or become a "famous-name" global Christian ministry. Too much publicity actually hinders the work.

To the Great Hall of the People

The change of name also played a part in our eventual entry into the People's Republic of China. I secured a visa to visit Beijing and Shanghai in 1984. Several couples had agreed to go with me, among them Paul J. Meyer and his wife Jane. They are experienced travelers and micro-managers of time. Which is why they asked me for an itinerary.

"We have none," I said.

Paul clarified his question. *"I mean what is the schedule?"*

"There is no schedule."

He looked perplexed.

"So what's your plan?"

My plan consisted of a small piece of paper bearing the name Madam Tu Zhen. At the request of the PRC leadership, this Chinese scholar and educator had recently overseen a visit by some of America's Fortune 500 company CEOs, traveling with them from Guangzhou to Beijing. I called her. Madam Tu Zhen kindly accepted my invitation to meet for tea. I found her gracious, direct, fluent in English, and extremely knowledgeable. She introduced me to her husband, also a recognized scholar and the son of the founder of the China Opera Company, Dr. Mei Lanfang.

The only request I made of Madam Tu Zhen that afternoon was that, if possible, she might introduce me to some other key players in Beijing. Within 36 hours I had enough meetings to fill up an entire month. Madam Tu Zhen commended me to leaders in the arts, education and the professions. She also arranged meetings with equivalent leaders in Shanghai. When we left China, all of the contacts we'd made insisted that we return.

Out of these friendships Haggai Institute formed in China came the opportunity to work as a Christian organization not only with Chinese Christian leaders but also with members of the national government. In 1988, I invited thirty-two key leaders from the PRC to take part in a Sino-American Cultural Exchange which Haggai Institute sponsored at Georgia's Lake Lanier. The first group came under the aegis of the CAAIF (China Association for the Advancement of International Friendship). It included mainly people in education, business, photojournalism, and the arts. The second group, representing the CAIFC (China Association for International Friendly Contact) included veteran government leaders. The PRC's first representative on the United Nations Security Council headed the group. He and his charming wife, also an experienced ambassador, made a powerful impact on the Americans involved in the event.

Since that time, many of China's most distinguished leaders have taken part in Haggai Institute's advanced leadership seminars – leaders both from government circles and from China's re-emerging Church. After twenty-seven visits to the country, I am honored – and not a little humbled –

Tony Chi. Vice President Training and Development, Singapore. Tony built the Wesley Methodist Church in Singapore to mega-church proportions, then pastored the Wesley Mission in Sydney, Australia, where he gave oversight to twelve congregations and was part of a team who built a $280 million church complex. He was elected the New South Wales Moderator of the Uniting Church in Australia.

that both leadership and press in the PRC have referred to me publicly as *lao pengyou*, "old friend."

The number of unevangelized in China exceeds the total population of North America, South America, and most of Africa combined. God is doing a great work in China, and Haggai Institute continues to be part of it.

What gives Haggai Institute its worldwide impact?

The Gospel never changes. But the methods used for transmitting it do change and must change. In 1955, World Vision President Bob Pierce met Jawaharlal Nehru, Prime Minister of that other massive nation, India. Nehru asked him, *"Dr. Pierce, do you believe that Christianity is self-propagating?"*

Bob responded with an emphatic, *"Of course."*

"Are you aware, Dr. Pierce, that the apostle Thomas brought Christianity to India's Malabar Coast in A.D. 52?"

"Yes, and I am aware that he died in India, where tradition tells us he was slain by a dart in the vicinity of Madras."

"That's correct," said Nehru. *"Now my question is: If Christianity is self-propagating, and if Christianity came to India more than 1,900 years ago, why do you find it necessary to prop up your religion with 9,000 foreign missionaries today?"*

It was a sign of things to come. When Dr. Rebekah Naylor finishes her stint in India, the Southern Baptist Mission Board, with the largest single missions budget in the world, will have no missionaries left in India. India doesn't want missionaries. Indeed the day of evangelism by missionary has long since passed. Never mind India; to send missionaries even to Bangladesh in the same proportion as there are ministers to population in

GUY RUTLAND, JR. In 1934, Guy Rutland set his goal to make a million dollars within a year of graduating. He succeeded, and went on to become an exemplary donor, giving multiplied millions to the cause of Christ, while maintaining a modest personal lifestyle.

America would require a force of 200,000 – at a cost of around $10 billion annually. That's at least seven times more than all the North American mission budgets put together. And that's to cover just one nation.

Demographics, economics, and diplomacy all argue against persisting with the old concept of missions. Dr. Paul Hiebert, world-renowned missiologist, has said that training nationals to evangelize nationals surpasses in effectiveness traditional foreign methods. *"Haggai Institute,"* he adds, *"is the only post-colonial model of missions I know."* It's also far less expensive. And it sidesteps the awkward problems raised when the citizens of one sovereign nation enter another with the aim of proselytizing their faith. That, in summary, is why Haggai Institute meets such a pressing need.

Haggai Institute does not plant Churches. We do not publish Bibles, sponsor orphans, distribute food, organize seminars on labor-management relations, nor underwrite specialized research in systematic theology. We have one aim: to provide the highest quality training in evangelism and leadership for national leaders. The leaders do the evangelism – and much else besides – and do it with national funding and with national personnel.

The program

What does Haggai Institute training look like, close up?

The sessions vary in length. Originally they lasted five weeks. The ever-faster pace of life, however, has forced us to reduce most to four, and some even to ten days. In addition, we run several three-week sessions – for women with family commitments, and in August, for educators with upcoming semesters. Occasionally we run special 14-day leadership seminars for top business

ELSA PRINCE BROEKHUIZEN. A woman of wealth and culture, Elsa Prince Broekhuizen has channeled substantial gifts, time, and influence into the Lord's work. She helped pay off the mortgage on the Maui Center.

people whose responsibilities prevent them taking more time away.

As preparation we ask participants to read this book. They are also required to submit a 2,500-word summary of their background: their country, its religions, how Christianity grew there, the nature of their work and ministry, what their aspirations are, and what they expect to gain from the H.I. program.

At both centers the teaching method is interactive. This isn't the sort of training where a superior imparts his wisdom and everyone else humbly takes notes. Faculty members suggest a direction for discussion, share their particular expertise, then serve as a catalyst for debate, study, and the writing of session reports. With a few exceptions, the faculty is drawn exclusively from the non-Western world. More than 150 are on the roster, from which ten to fourteen will be brought in to cover the core subjects. Some are full-time; others are "on call" or brought in to cover specialist topics as needed.

We pack in as much as the available time will hold. Classes run Monday to Saturday from 8:15 a.m. to around 9:00 p.m. (5:00 p.m. on Saturdays), each day being divided into five lecture periods of one hour and fifteen minutes. Morning devotions take 35 minutes daily, though participants often get together themselves for prayer after the teaching time ends. The schedule is intense. The seminar has the participants up at 6:30 in the morning, and to bed no earlier than 10:00 at night. They enjoy a brief rest period between the noon meal and the 3:00 p.m. session in the afternoon; and, in the longer seminars at least, a day is set apart for sight-seeing and shopping.

That participants are willing to discipline themselves in this way is a mark of their caliber. Characteristically a seminar group will bring together a cross-section of professions: lawyers,

JOHN AND JEANNE ALLEN.
First elected to the Board in 1985, John Allen served as project manager for the renovation of the Mid-Pacific Center in 2001. He and his wife Jeanne are a multi-talented couple who have combined their enormous skills for the benefit of the Haggai program.

doctors, dentists, government officials and ministers, university presidents, professors, high court justices, psychologists, multinational businessmen, architects, Bible translators, and all levels of clergy from pastors to archbishops. Some have doctorates, some have degrees, some are qualified in quite different ways. They gather as proven leaders, able to inspire one another from their varied positions of expertise, ready to refine their leadership skills. They leave as trained evangelists, ready to apply their newly refined powers of leadership to the service of the Gospel. ■

The Great Wall.
So long isolated from the rest of the world, China is now looking outward.

"Leadership training is the key point in mission work," says Dr. (Bishop) Sundo Kim, Senior Pastor of Korea's Kwanglim Methodist Church. "Without trained leaders there is no effective church."

In 1971, Kwanglim Church had just 150 members. Today, under Sundo Kim's leadership, its membership roll is close to 100,000. Kwanglim has four satellite church campuses and a growing number of daughter churches. More than 1,200 prayer cell groups undergird this varied ministry.

Sundo Kim is also director of, and the creative spirit behind, the Kwanglim World Prayer Center, a place of quiet retreat with overnight accommodations for 800.

The training Sundo Kim received at Haggai Institute in 1987 played a key role in this success. The H.I. experience led him to develop a strong base of leadership from within his congregation. He credits H.I. with accelerating the church's global vision and outreach. Kwanglim Church is involved in ministry in China, Japan, the Philippines, Russia, Brazil and Zimbabwe.

"I pray that Haggai Institute will continue to train leaders from all over the world. We really appreciate Haggai Institute. Thank you for your contribution to the work of the Lord in Korea."

6 The Funding Philosophy

Haggai Institute owes its effectiveness to countless visionary men and women who continue and expand its work. Advanced leadership training doesn't come cheap. The truth of the matter is, it costs $9,600 for every leader who attends a session. Of this amount, the participant pays $500 of his own money (two months' salary – or more – in some nations). The rest is made available through private donations.

Costs break down into these main components:

JOHN BOLTEN. Business leader and world citizen, John Bolten has used his considerable influence on behalf of the H.I. ministry since 1982. He and his wife Ines make their home in Germany and Chile.

- AIR TRAVEL. Almost every participant and faculty member has to be flown in from his or her home country, sometimes as much as 10,000 miles away. In some countries, overseas air tickets attract a 100 percent tax.

- ROOM AND BOARD. Maximizing session effectiveness requires high quality service and accommodation.

- FOLLOW-UP. For at least ten years after a participant leaves, Haggai Institute stays in contact to offer counsel and support in his or her work of reaching others with the Gospel.

- LOCATING/SCREENING. All participants have to be checked out before admittance to the program, and Haggai Institute engages several full-time professionals to accomplish this.

- EDUCATIONAL COSTS. Haggai Institute uses only top-class faculty. In addition, we provide materials and classroom facilities, and an "advance pack" mailed out beforehand to allow the participant to prepare adequately.

- ADMINISTRATIVE SUPPORT. In order to maintain the training sessions and ensure funding, Haggai Institute employs a small and highly professional body of administrative staff.

The money goes a long, long way

In 1986, John Bolten, a German-born American businessman, and Frank Olsen, American Broadcasting Company's head writer for 14 years, accompanied me on a round-the-world trip that included Indonesia. Here I introduced them to Dr. S.J. Sutjiono, who completed his Haggai Institute training in 1970. Here are the highlights of Sutjiono's ministry in the intervening years. By 1986:

Dr. Won Sul Lee. Later President of Han Nam University in Taejon, Korea, Won Sul Lee brought his considerable influence and prestige to bear in the role of H.I. Faculty Chairman until 1981.

- He'd trained more than 16,000 Indonesian leaders, both lay people and clergy, who work for the Lord on Indonesia's 3,000 inhabited islands.

- He'd founded a Church with a present membership in excess of 24,000.

- He'd written 30 major books. Some are for Christians, and some for the general public. Several were produced as follow-up for the 16,000 he has trained.

- He'd been lecturing in seven different departments at Indonesia's most prestigious university.

John Bolten made the point that if you divide the cost of a $9,100 sponsorship by the 16,000 Sutjiono had trained, then divide it further by the innumerable decisions for Christ that have followed these new evangelists, then the Haggai Institute method must be one of the most cost-effective means of furthering the Gospel known today. And that represents the work of only *one* Haggai Institute graduate.

Contrast this with the costs of conventional missionary work. It is impossible to support a missionary couple in any city of the world today – whether it be Lagos, Jakarta, or Karachi – for less than $100,000. But let's assume for a moment that it cost only *half* that much. To support 43,000 missionaries (the number trained through H.I. at the time of writing – April 2002) would require $2,150,000,000 per annum – significantly more than the total amount of money spent on non-Western missions by all North American Churches, Protestant and Catholic. And every fourth year those 43,000 missionaries would all be home on furlough.

In Brazil, Dr. **EDELTO ANTUNES** left a lucrative career in dental surgery to become a full-time pastor. He developed his gift for evangelism at **Haggai Institute** and has subsequently trained over 4,000 others.

Why go for big givers?

Every other month, for I don't know how many years, Mr C.C. Parkman, a pensioner from Fort Worth, Texas, used to send me $3.00 and a two-sided, almost illegible letter. It cost more than $3.00 to receipt a gift. And I must have totaled hours trying to decipher his handwriting. Having said that, I still think of Mr Parkman as one of the biggest donors in the history of H.I. Why? His insights, commitment, and encouragement could not have been bought with any amount of money.

So I thank God for every gift we receive, small or great. And I know that many organizations rely on small donors. After all, it can be advantageous to have a million people give you $5.00 a year – you spread your risk, and you don't get hit if one drops out. On the other hand, you are considerably increasing your overhead, and distancing yourself from your donor base. Haggai Institute, then, avoids a big operation of tearing open envelopes, and concentrates its energies instead on a smaller number of loyal supporters – individuals, Churches, and foundations. Our approach is to find people who have not only the vision to support Haggai Institute's unique ministry, but the financial resources to make an impact on world missions.

I believe strongly in personal contact between those at the cutting edge of ministry and those who work to support it. It was Henry F. "Hank" McCamish, one of my "guardian angels" in the early days, who underlined to me that you don't need a crowd of people – you need the *right* people. That is why I travel so many thousands of miles a year to keep relationships strong.

Rev. Reginaldo André Kruklis (right) interpreting for Dr. John Haggai at Lagoinha Baptist Church in Belo Horizonte, Brazil. Rev. Márcio Valadão (1991 alumnus) is the senior pastor of the 22,000-member church. A supremely gifted leader, Reginaldo became president of Haggai Institute in August 2001.

Absolute transparency

The late 1980s saw a rash of financial scandals involving Christian ministries. In my view Christian organizations have a sacred obligation to expend monies on the projects for which they were given. If money given to publish Bibles is used instead to build an orphanage, that is wrong. In the business world they call it misappropriation of funds, and you go to jail.

During a live broadcast on Paraguay's Radio Odedira. The host is OSCAR VASQUEZ (right). Dr. NORIVAL TRINDADE (center) acts as interpreter.

For that reason, Haggai Institute maintains a policy of strict openness. We believe that heads of Christian ministries should be subject to the same kinds of financial scrutiny as U.S. political candidates. All income and perks should be disclosed, including:

- salaries

- retirement benefits

- housing

- automobiles and airplanes

- club memberships

- charge accounts paid by the organization

- hospital and income replacement insurance

- income and perks distributed to spouse and family members

**JIM AND OPAL MCCORMICK.
The $7,000 contributed by
Jim McCormick and his wife
Opal led to the incorporation
of the ministry in 1962,
making possible what later
became Haggai Institute.**

- income from board
  memberships

- royalties on materials
  produced and
  distributed by the
  organization

- costs to the
  organization of
  sabbaticals
  or long-term absences

- gifts of money,
  property, or materials.

In proof of this, we believe,
Christian ministry heads
should be ready to disclose,
to policing agencies like the
ECFA and to major donors,
their last three income tax
statements and their current
net worth. When you ask
others to support you
financially, you owe it to
them to demonstrate that
incoming funds are going
where they're meant to go –
not least because in many
countries, as is the case in
the U.S., Christian
ministries enjoy tax-exempt
status. No one whose
income derives from the
public media has a right to
keep financial transactions
hidden – and certainly not
a representative of the Most
High God. ∎

Kwabena Darko GHANA

Kwabena Darko operates one of Ghana's most elaborate and profitable enterprises, Darko Farms & Co. Ltd. He has run for President. He has also trained an estimated 20,000 Christian leaders for evangelism on the continent of Africa.

"The Haggai Institute training really opened my eyes," he says. "It helped me understand the essentials of leadership. It motivated me to evangelize. It has taught me to set goals and to pray about those goals. I have practiced what I've learned. I've applied it, and it works."

One of the first things he did on his return from the seminar was to turn over thirty minutes of company time to Bible study, counseling and praise – often leading the sessions himself. Since then he has had no industrial unrest and labor turnover has gone down. He calls his employees "partners in progress."

Beyond the workplace he has used his motivation training gained at H.I. to build the Full Gospel Businessmen's Fellowship in Ghana from five chapters to 180. His international networking has allowed him to reach professionals with the Gospel in more than 30 countries. And he has begun the nonprofit Kwabena Darko Foundation to give other Ghanaians the skill to build business – as he did – from almost nothing.

7 Frequently Asked Questions

People who encounter Haggai Institute for the first time often ask searching questions of our methods. Here are some of the "frequently asked questions" and the answers we give:

"Why focus on rapid evangelism?"

There's a saying you hear occasionally in more traditional Churches: *"Oh, we don't want mushroom growth – we want solid growth."*

Sometimes this reflects a valid concern about turning converts into disciples. What counts, they say, isn't how many you can get into a Church, but how many you can keep. The answer, though, isn't to limit your rate of growth. It's to design ways of making rapid growth effective.

Have they not heard of the 3,000 souls saved in one day at Pentecost? Or the 5,000 saved at the one service mentioned in Acts 4? Or the two entire cities – Sharon and Lydda – that turned to Christ under the preaching of the apostle Peter?

With TITO SAGUIER, President of the Senate of Paraguay (far right). In the background (left to right) are Dr. NORIVAL TRINDADE, Dr. HEINRICH RATZLAFF, H.I. alumnus and Paraguayan congressman, and the then H.I. President Dr. WILLIAM M. HINSON.

We should not dismiss these as peculiarities of the early Church. Not long ago, 30,000 people turned to the Lord every week under the anointed preaching of Dr. John Sung. Korea's Young Nak Church grew from 27 refugees to 65,000 in 40 years. In just 13 years, Seoul's Yoido Full Gospel Church grew from five members to over half a million.

THE HAGGAI INSTITUTE STORY

Rapid expansion of the Church does not mean superficial conversion of the members. Christ lays down the challenge to take such action as will make a plausible impact on population growth. And listen to this staggering word from our Lord: *"The works that I do shall you do, and greater than these shall you do, because I go to my Father."* Haggai Institute aims to obey.

"Isn't Haggai Institute elitist?"

Western missionary organizations have been fond of saying that H.I. concentrates attention only on the higher socio-economic groups in the countries from which we select participants. Why, they ask, do we neglect the "ordinary" people? Isn't that unfair?

You might ask, of course, whether it's fair to present the Gospel to "ordinary" people through a Western missionary when it can be presented more effectively through someone who belongs to the local culture and knows its language and customs. Yes, we are elitist – but only in the sense that we see our role under God as facilitating more telling evangelism.

We aim for the select few who can give the "leading edge" in proclaiming the Gospel of the Lord Jesus Christ to the masses. All Haggai Institute alumni have demonstrated proven leadership ability. We reason that, if they have been successful in leading their compatriots in business, law, medicine, or any other secular discipline, they will have the ability to provide leadership for evangelism as well.

Must we ignore the needs of 2.25 billion people who have yet to hear about Jesus, just to gain the support of a small coterie of Western believers in the mission apparatus who look on any innovative program as a threat to Christian unity? Who are really the elitists?

"The works that I do shall you do."

"Isn't Haggai Institute too small to make a difference?"

Well, an organization represented in over 150 countries can't be *that* small. Still, I had someone ask me recently how many participants attend an H.I. session. When I replied "twenty-five," he turned his nose up and informed me that a seminar run by his own organization had recently attracted 12,000.

But probe this a little. How were those 12,000 selected? What did they actually gain from the seminar? What was the quality of the training given – and who gave it? Did the seminar have any discernible impact on later evangelism, or is the 12,000 attendance figure a self-justifying end?

Against such questions I can guarantee that every single member of the twenty-five attending a Haggai Institute seminar will be hand-picked, qualified, and committed to carry both training and evangelism forward and to reproduce other leaders. Also, how can you have interactive training with 12,000 people? That issue alone is crucial, because strong and motivated alumni will pass their training on as promised, making the total number of session beneficiaries not 25 but 2,500 – and quite possibly more. Nor is this training thrown indiscriminately at a mass of casual inquirers. It's a targeted, well-honed, and effective program going to people who made sacrifices to get it.

DOT and POLLY POOLE, with (center) the first H.I. Dean, Dr. ERNEST WATSON. Polly Poole first encountered H.I. in 1976. He took the trouble to observe the training in person, and has consistently given generously of his funds and leadership skills.

"How do you know your alumni will perform?"

The leader of one of America's most blessed parachurch organizations once asked former H.I. Vice President Doug Cozart, *"What control does John Haggai have on the leaders when they return to their respective nations?"*

Doug didn't budge an inch. Instead, he responded, *"The same control your seminary has had on you since you graduated."*

The desire to "control" is exactly what's wrong with traditional Western missions. Haggai Institute doesn't set out to control people. It selects candidates who share a passion for world evangelism. It equips them. And then it gives them the hand of fellowship as they go out to do whatever work God is leading them into.

Can we guarantee that every alumnus will keep his or her commitment to pass on the training to a hundred others? Of course not. But the fact is that most of them do. And many far exceed that number.

With the late Egyptian President ANWAR SADAT, one of several national leaders to have acknowledged the work of Haggai Institute.

Vera Vassilieff, for instance, came to Haggai Institute as a wife and mother of three children, as an associate professor in pharmacology, an internationally published researcher in medicine, winner of national awards for research, and as an active member of her local Church.

She recalls, *"I was very insecure about my personal role and responsibility in the leadership ministry which God has given me."* Yet in the first year following her session at Singapore, Dr. Vassilieff held a training seminar for 50 Sunday School teachers from Churches in five cities around São Paulo, Brazil. She shared her Haggai Institute leadership training with 120 ministers and Church elders at a Christian leadership conference. And she presented the program *Being a Leader* to an audience of over 400.

"Is Haggai Institute really unique?"

One morning in 1976, Cecil Day invited me to breakfast with one of the world's most respected mission leaders – a man I had admired for years. As we sat in Cecil's private dining room, the mission leader insisted that his denomination had been training leaders in the developing world for a hundred years.

I knew he was mistaken. I knew the mission philosophy of his denomination. But out of respect for Cecil I said nothing. Before my cup of coffee grew cold, I thought to myself, *"Well, there goes Cecil's support of Haggai Institute."*

Later that afternoon I bumped into Cecil in an elevator. A man of few words, Cecil looked at me and said, *"Thanks for joining me at breakfast, John."* Then he paused and added, *"They just don't understand, do they?"*

Very little has changed. Since Haggai Institute took the initiative, a number of other mission groups have jumped on the bandwagon. It's very easy to say you're doing training for evangelism. But analyze what these groups are actually doing, and you'll quickly see the differences. The fact is, no other organization has the same stringent selection procedure, has the same quality of participants, is active in as many countries, is as sensitive to culture and geopolitics, or is as downright effective.

As one hard-nosed businessman said, *"I don't support Haggai Institute because I like John Haggai, or because I admire the way the organization is run. I support it because after travelling the world I see that the H.I. program is unique, and that it delivers more bang for the buck than I get in any other overseas ministry."*

Dr. CHANDU RAY.
A superlative Anglican bishop and evangelist who translated the Bible into Tibetan and Sindhi, Chandu Ray lectured at H.I. from 1971 and for many years headed the Singapore office and served as faculty anchorman for the international sessions. He also spearheaded H.I.'s expansion into Africa.

"Why doesn't Haggai Institute cooperate with other mission groups?"

Haggai Institute cooperates with many groups, but it does not align itself with other Western organizations – for two reasons.

First, to do so would discredit us with leaders outside the West who object to Western methods of addressing the evangelistic challenge. They understand what sets Haggai Institute apart, and value our expectation that indigenous Christians will take the lead in spreading the Gospel.

Second, in a rapidly changing world, the attitude of governments to Christianity in general and evangelism in particular can soon change. In some cases this means missionaries will be asked to leave. In other cases it means that national Christians will be put in jail for associating with foreigners. Staying free of other Western mission groups enables Haggai Institute to function freely where intrusive methods of evangelism are being resisted.

So partly out of principle, and partly for reasons of operational effectiveness, Haggai Institute works on its own. Many full-time missionaries see the wisdom of this. More often than I can remember, I've been quietly taken aside by missionaries in the field and told how much they wish their boards could see "what's really going on." Sadly, some mission heads have been away from the action for twenty years. Inevitably, they have lost touch with changing culture and demographics. And if mission heads lose touch, little can be done to communicate the realities of modern missions to the congregations who support the missionary effort.

Speaking on "The Authentic Leader" at the first ever Haggai Institute seminar in Hong Kong.

"What's next?"

Well, only God knows that. By His grace, and in little more than thirty years, Haggai Institute can claim to have redrawn the map of missions. According to theologian Dr. Carl F. Henry, *"By emphasizing leadership development for evangelism, Haggai Institute has pioneered in training nationals from many lands for indigenous as well as cross-cultural ministries. Both its program and international teaching staff have enjoyed well-deserved recognition."*

Such recognition has come from many quarters. Chuck Colson of Prison Fellowship International declared himself *"thrilled with the tremendous results"* achieved by Haggai Institute alumni. In his travels around the world, the late Dr. Norman Vincent Peale said he had many times *"encountered the strong and caring Christian influence of the Haggai Institute ministry of world evangelism."* Dr. Ted Engstrom, president emeritus of World Vision, describes the Haggai Institute program as *"a creative, innovative, refreshing approach to the key task of the Church worldwide."* We should regard it, adds Dr. D. James Kennedy, president of Evangelism Explosion International, as *"one of the great hopes of our time for the fulfilment of the Great Commission."*

Haggai Institute remains alert for God's voice in responding to the challenge of evangelism. The late W. B. Camp of Bakersfield, California, fourteen years an officer of the United States Chamber of Commerce, once said, *"You can't use yesterday's methods in today's world and still be in business tomorrow."* In missions, Haggai Institute, ever attentive to global changes, strives to remain not only on the leading edge, but a little ahead of it. A truly global Gospel demands nothing less. ∎

JOY D'ARATA. The first woman Chairman of the Haggai Institute International Board (2000–2002). A global traveler, she has served in the field of philanthropy for more than twenty years.

INDEX